CW00669615

Published by Collins
An imprint of HarperCollins Publishers
Westerhill Road, Bishopbriggs,
Glasgow G64 2QT

HarperCollins Publishers
1st Floor, Watermarque Building,
Ringsend Road, Dublin 4, Ireland

www.harpercollins.co.uk

I dedicate this book to my Camp Friendship friends, the kindest people I know.

© HarperCollins Publishers 2022

Collins® is a registered trademark of HarperCollins Publishers Ltd.

All images © Shutterstock.com

Text © Becky Goddard-Hill

Cover title font © Kia Marie Hunt

Cover author name font and bee illustration
on cover, p.3 and p.5 © Clare Forrest

All rights reserved. No part of this publication may be
reproduced, stored in a retrieval system, or transmitted,
in any form or by any means, electronic, mechanical,
photocopying, recording or otherwise without the prior
permission in writing of the Publisher and copyright
owners. The contents of this publication are believed
correct at the time of printing. Nevertheless the Publisher
can accept no responsibility for errors or omissions,
changes in the detail given or for any expense or loss
thereby caused.

A catalogue record for this book is available from the
British Library.

978-0-00-854523-9

Printed in India

10 9 8 7 6 5 4 3 2 1

MIX
Paper from
responsible sources
FSC™ C007454

FSC
www.fsc.org

This book is produced from independently certified FSC™ paper
to ensure responsible forest management.

For more information visit: www.harpercollins.co.uk/green

Collins

365 Days of kind

Becky Goddard-Hill

kind

KINDNESS is POWERFUL, it can HEAL, HELP, ENCOURAGE and SUPPORT. And, whether that KINDNESS is shown to yourself, other PEOPLE or THE PLANET, it makes a HUGE and positive DIFFERENCE in **YOUR LIFE.**

Are you ready to spread
kindness every day of the year?

Try out the simple activities
throughout your day or the
whole week through and read
the inspirational quotes all about
being kind. The affirmations
are positive statements that
you might want to repeat
to yourself or say aloud to
strengthen your belief in them.

The book is perfect for opening
at the beginning of your day,
before you go to bed or anytime!

NEW BEGINNINGS

1 A new book and a new beginning with 365 days of kindness ahead of you. Could you make a kindness commitment for the year ahead? Perhaps it could be to use more kind words, or to be kinder to others or yourself? Try writing it and signing your name against it. Then place it somewhere you will see it often.

IT'S A TIME FOR NEW BEGINNINGS.

2

I will fill the YEAR AHEAD with KINDNESS.

3

> **"** I hope you realise that every day is a fresh start for you. That every sunrise is a new chapter in your life waiting to be written. **"**

Juansen Dizon

4 "Where do we BEGIN? BEGIN with the HEART."

Julian of Norwich

> "We all get the exact same 365 DAYS. The only difference is what we do with them."
>
> Hillary DePiano

5

6 I commit to being
KINDER.

7 "TO KINDNESS AND LOVE, the things we need the most."

The Grinch

Kind People

8

Can you name the top 10 kindest people you know? Stay close – they will treat you well and help you become kinder too. Kindness is contagious.

9

"Try to be a rainbow in someone else's cloud."

Maya Angelou

10

I stay close to kind people.

11

"You will never have a completely bad day if you show kindness at least once."

Greg Henry Quinn

12

"Be kind, BE HONEST, be loving, BE TRUE and all of these things will come back to you."

I am a kind PERSON. 13

14 "KIND PEOPLE are the best kind of PEOPLE."

Kindness is Important

15 How important is kindness in your life? If it has slipped behind being popular, funny, friendly or clever in your list of values then it's time to promote it back to number 1. Can you make a MASSIVE 'be kind' poster to place on your bedroom door so you get the message LOUD and clear? Or how about making 'be kind' post-it notes and plastering them all over your fridge? Let's keep it at the front of our minds and our actions.

16
I know **KINDNESS** is important. ♪

17
"WHATEVER you want to be when you grow up, be KIND." ☆

18 "Three things in **HUMAN LIFE** are important: the first is to be kind; the second is to be **KIND**, and the third is to be **KIND**."

Henry James

19 "KINDNESS ♪ is the new COOL." ☆

20 "It's nice to be IMPORTANT, but it's more IMPORTANT to be nice."

21 I put **KINDNESS** first. ♪

SELF KINDNESS

22

A 'self-kindness' is an act you do to support, encourage or soothe yourself. It is important you build self-kindness into every day and then when times are tough you know exactly how to make yourself feel better.

Can you create a little diary for the week with a 'self-kindness' plotted in for each day? You could include:

- *Watching my favourite TV show*
- *Phoning grandma*
- *Doing some baking*
- *Having a lovely long lie in*
- *Listening to some top tunes*

23 *I talk to myself ✻ with love.*

24 "An empty lantern provides no light. Self-care is the fuel that allows your light to shine brightly."

25

" Be kind to yourself so you can be happy enough to be kind to the world. "

Misha Collins

26

" I always **DESERVE** the best **TREATMENT** because I never put up with any other. "

Emma, *Emma*

I am kind to MYSELF. **27**

28

"If you make friends with yourself you will never be alone."

Maxwell Maltz

Kindness to Others

29 Do something kind today for every person who lives in your home – it could be a tiny thing but think of each person and do something that you know will make them smile.

30

" **Unless we think of others and do something for them, we miss one of the greatest sources of HAPPINESS.** "

Ray Lyman Wilbur

31

I treat others as I would like them to TREAT ME.

"That's **WHAT I** consider true **GENEROSITY:** you give **YOUR** all, and yet you **ALWAYS** feel as if it costs you **NOTHING.**"

Simone de Beauvoir

33 " You will discover that you have two hands. One is for helping yourself and the other is for helping others. "
Sam Levenson

34 "Life's most persistent and urgent question is, 'What are you doing for others?' "
Martin Luther King Jr.

35 I am kind to my FAMILY.

Kind Words

36

There are so many words that mean kindness, can you think of 7? I'll start you off, how about 'caring'?

37

" Kind words can be short and easy to speak, but their echoes are truly endless. "

Mother Teresa

My words are powerful, so I use them carefully.

38

39

66 Good words are worth much and cost little. 99

George Herbert

40

66 Our WORDS should be PURRS instead of HISSES. 99

Kathrine Palmer Peterson

"A kind word is like a SPRING DAY." 41

Russian proverb

42

I use kind WORDS.

Kind Thoughts

43

When unkind thoughts float into your mind, you have the power to say stop and give them no attention. Then you can choose a kinder way to think about something. If you find that hard, clam down first then try again.

Ask for help if you are struggling and use your affirmations. Looking at something through kind, understanding eyes can make such a difference.

It's not easy to change how you think, but it is worth it.

Have you had any unkind thoughts recently that you want to change?

44

"*If you judge people, you have no time to love them.*"

Mother Teresa

45

My **kindness** is bigger than my judgment.

46

"We don't see things as they are, we see them as we are."

Anaïs Nin

47

"Life doesn't require that we be the best, only that we try our best."

H. Jackson Brown Jr.

48 "Be someone's **SUNSHINE** when their **SKIES** are **GREY**."

49 I think kind **THOUGHTS**.

Empathy

50 ♪

Think about someone you know who is having a hard time. Take a look at how the world appears through their eyes. Imagine how they might feel. This is empathy. Can you reach out to them in some way?

BEING EMPATHIC (SEEING SOMEONE ELSE'S WORLD) ALMOST ALWAYS LEADS TO AN INCREASE IN KINDNESS.

51

I listen to other people and hear how THEY FEEL.

52

"See the LIGHT in each other. Be the light for EACH OTHER."

53

"EMPATHY

is seeing with the eyes of another, listening with the ears of another, and feeling with the heart of another.

> " Empathy is simply listening, holding space, withholding judgment, emotionally connecting, and communicating that incredibly healing message of 'you're not alone.' "

54

Brené Brown

55 > " There are two types of people, those who come into a room and say, 'well here am I' and those who come in and say 'ah there you are'. "

Frederick Collins

56 I try and see things through other **PEOPLE'S EYES.**

COMPLIMENTS

57

Hello wonderful you. I have some free compliments for you. Will you please pass them out today, one per person.

- You look amazing.
- You are so lovely.
- I think you are such a kind person.
- You always make me smile.
- It's always great to see you.
- You are fantastic, I'm so glad you are my friend.

"One compliment can keep me going for a whole week."

Mark Twain

58

I use my words to make others feel good.

59

60

" **A compliment is VERBAL SUNSHINE.** "

Atharva Veda

61

" **COMPLIMENT people. Magnify their STRENGTHS, not their WEAKNESSES.** "

Joyce Meyer

I am 62 GENEROUS with COMPLIMENTS.

63

"It's good to receive compliments, and it's even better to give them."

Jason Harvey

Friendship

Think about your 3 favourite friends. Aren't they amazing? What could you do for each of those friends that they would really appreciate? Go do it!

64

65

I AM THANKFUL FOR MY FRIENDSHIPS.

☆

66

" There is nothing on this earth more to be prized than true friendship. "

St. Thomas Aquinas

⁶⁷"**A FRIEND** is one of the **NICEST THINGS** you can have and one of the **BEST THINGS** you can be."

68 "A kind friend is the right kind of friend."

69 "Many people will walk in and out of your life, but only true friends leave footprints in your heart."

Eleanor Roosevelt

70 I am **KIND** to my friends.

PASS IT ON

71

Think about the last person who was kind to you and about what they said or did. Who could you pass a similar kindness on to today?

It's always good to pass kindness on.

72 "What goes around comes around – so be kind."

73 I spread KINDNESS.

74

"A bit of fragrance always clings to the hand that gives roses."

Chinese proverb

75

"Lose YOURSELF in GENEROUS service and every day can be a most unusual day, a TRIUMPHANT day, an abundantly REWARDING day!"

William Arthur Ward

76

I pass KINDNESS on.

77

"The point is not to pay back kindness but to pass it on."

Julia Alvarez

Giving

78 ☆

What could you give
away today? Could
it be a compliment,
an hour of your time,
a game you have
outgrown?
Check in with yourself
how it feels when you
give something away.
I think you will find
you are smiling.

79

"GENEROSITY takes an open HEART and a LOVE that asks for nothing in return."

♪ **80**

I AM GENEROUS.

81

"**KINDNESS** in words creates **CONFIDENCE.** **KINDNESS** in thinking creates **PROFOUNDNESS.** Kindness in giving **CREATES LOVE."**

Lao Tzu

"Set your heart on doing good. Do it over and over again and you will be filled with joy."

82

Buddha.

"For it is in giving that we receive."

83

St. Francis of Assisi

84 I have a
LOT TO GIVE.

Kindness Makes Us Happy

85

Can you remember a time when you were kind to someone and a time when someone was kind to you? Tell someone about those times or write them down and catch yourself smiling at your memories. Kindness makes us happy.

86

"With kindness, we all rise."

87

Kindness makes other people happy.

88

" Remember that the happiest people are not those getting more, but those giving more. "

Robin Sharma

89

" PLANT seeds of HAPPINESS, hope, SUCCESS, and LOVE; it will all come back to you in ABUNDANCE. This is the law of NATURE. "

Steve Maraboli

Kindness makes me HAPPY.

90

91

"Someday you will find out that there is far more happiness in another's happiness than in your own."

Honoré de Balzac

LOVE

92

Can you
fill in the gaps?
I believe love is ...
And ways I can
show it are ...

93

66 *Do what you can, with what you have, where you are.* 99

Theodore Roosevelt

94

I show ♪ my love.

95

"Every time you smile at someone, it is an action of love, a gift to that person, a beautiful thing."

Mother Teresa

96

"LOVE yourself first, and everything else FALLS in line. You really have to love YOURSELF to get ANYTHING done in this WORLD."

Lucille Ball

I am full of LOVE. 97

98

"It's not how much we give but how much love we put into giving."

Mother Teresa

Beautiful
Kindness

99 ♪

Kindness truly is the most
beautiful thing in the world.
Close your eyes and see the
face of the kindest person
you know. Aren't they
beautiful?
Whenever you feel fed up
with life just thinking about
kind people or kind actions
will give you a lift.
Kindness is very precious
and taking a moment to
appreciate its beauty puts us
all in a good mood.

100

MY KINDNESS IS A ☆ BEAUTIFUL GIFT.

101

"Kindness is like snow – it beautifies everything it covers."

Kahlil Gibran

102

"**FOR BEAUTIFUL** eyes, look for the good in others; for **BEAUTIFUL LIPS,** speak only words of **KINDNESS;** and for poise, walk with the **KNOWLEDGE** that you are never alone."

Audrey Hepburn

103 " It's the most beautiful job in the world to give happiness to people. "

Hubert de Givenchy

104 "Kindness is a beauty that **NEVER FADES**."

105 I see the **BEAUTY** in kindness.

ACTS OF KINDNESS

106

Think about someone who guides you and how much they look out for you. It is time to give back. It might be a grown up you live with, a teacher or a coach. Now think of an act of kindness you could do for that person who matters to you so much.

Perhaps it is a chore of some kind, it could be giving them a thank you card, baking them a treat, or arranging a lovely surprise. What could you do for them today?

"No act of kindness, no matter how small, is ever wasted."

107

Aesop

I put my kindness into action.

108

109

"We are made kind by being kind."

Eric Hoffer

110

"REMEMBER there is no such thing as a small act of KINDNESS. Every act creates a RIPPLE with no LOGICAL end."

Scott Adams

I am kind and thoughtful.

111

112

"Sometimes it takes only one act of kindness and caring to change a person's life."

Jackie Chan

Hugs

113

Hugs can be amazing. They can feel lovely, warm supportive and squishy and tell people that you care about them. Sometimes sadly people we want to hug are too far away.

Can you think of a brilliant way to send them a 'sort of hug' from a distance today?

I bet you can.

(*Don't forget if you don't want to hug someone that is always okay and if they don't want to be hugged then that's always cool too.)

114

I CAN SHARE HOW MUCH I CARE.

115

"The best gift you can give is a hug: one size fits all and no one ever minds if you return it."

Marge Piercy

☆ 116

"PEOPLE will forget what you said, people will FORGET what you did, but people will NEVER FORGET how you made them FEEL."

Maya Angelou

"A hug is a smile with arms, a laugh with a stronger grip."

117

Terri Guillemets

118

"There is something in a simple hug that always warms the heart. It welcomes us back home and makes it easier to part."

Johnny Ray Ryder Jr.

I can hug myself (said whilst hugging yourself).

119

THANK YOU

120

When someone shows us kindness, giving thanks is important. Not only does it encourage them to be kind to someone else, but it also lets them know how much we value their kindness. Who do you need to say thank you to that perhaps you missed? How are you going to do it – a note, a text, in person, a letter, or with a small homemade gift?

121

I show how grateful I am.

"Silent gratitude isn't very much to anyone."

122

Gertrude Stein

123

Appreciation can make a day, even change a life. Your willingness to put it into words is all that is necessary. "

Margaret Cousins

124

" The HEART that gives THANKS is a HAPPY one, for we cannot feel THANKFUL and UNHAPPY at the same time. "

Douglas Wood

I am **THANKFUL** for all the **KINDNESS** I am shown. **125**

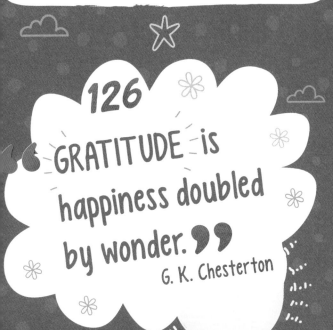

126

"**GRATITUDE** is happiness doubled by wonder."

G. K. Chesterton

Kindness
Touches Everyone

127 ✳

Kindness touches everyone, no matter what age or gender, no matter where someone lives or what language they speak. It is amazing and it is universal. Try saying 'I am kind' in all the different languages below (pop onto Google translate if you want to know how to pronounce them). There is one for each day this week.

- *sunt bun (Romanian)*
- *ben kibarım (Turkish)*
- *nginomusa (Zulu)*
- *ich bin nett (German)*
- *ako ay mabait (Filipino)*
- *eu sou gentil (Portuguese)*
- *jag är snäll (Swedish)*

128

WHEREVER I GO I TAKE MY KINDNESS WITH ME.

129

"Everyone understands KINDNESS."

"When we HELP OURSELVES, we find moments of HAPPINESS. When we HELP OTHERS, we find LASTING FULFILMENT."

130

Simon Sinek

131 "Do your little bit of good where you are; it's those little bits of good put together that overwhelm the world."
Desmond Tutu

"One of the most important things you can do on this earth is to let people know they are not alone."
132 Shannon L. Alder

♪ I strive to be kind to **133**
EVERYONE.

Encouraging Others

134

Could you make a card for someone today to cheer them on – or if you'd rather talk, maybe you could call them up and send some encouraging words their way?

Whether your granny is learning to juggle, or your best friend is trying out for a new football team, a few words of encouragement will spur them on and be much appreciated.

135

How you make others feel about themselves says a lot about you.

136

I like to **CHEER** people on.

66 The unselfish effort to bring cheer to others will be the beginning of a happier life for ourselves. 99

137 Helen Keller

138

66 TODAY will never come again. Be a BLESSING. Be a friend. ENCOURAGE SOMEONE. Take time to care. Let your WORDS heal, and not WOUND. 99

I am 139
SUPPORTIVE.

140

"Love the trees until their leaves fall off, then encourage them to try again next year."

Chad Sugg

KINDNESS TO STRANGERS

141

An act of kindness for someone we don't know might sound like a strange thing to do but, everyone wins with kindness. You will make someone's day and feel brilliant yourself in the process.

Perhaps you leave little painted stones in your community for people to find with 'You Rock' written on. Or maybe you could make little bookmarks for your library books and leave them squirreled inside for strangers to find. Perhaps you could leave a joke on a postcard in a cafe.

I bet you have tons of great ideas.

"Always be a
little kinder
than necessary."
J. M. Barrie

I make the
world a
nicer place.

144

"Be kind whenever possible. It is always possible."

Dalai Lama

"It isn't WHAT we say or THINK that DEFINES us, but WHAT we do." **145**

I ENJOY MAKING PEOPLE SMILE. 146

147

"Practise random kindness and senseless acts of beauty."

Anne Herbert

Plant Kindness

148

Whatever you plant will bring
joy whether that's to passers-by,
birds, bees, or even your tummy.
Could you plant some cress, or
some sunflower seeds, perhaps
you could grow some wildflowers
or try your hand at potatoes?
If you can't plant anything,
could you pick a few dandelions
(where many grow) and make
dandelion honey? Or use a few
daisies to make a daisy chain
for someone?
Plants and kindness go
hand in hand.

149

I plant KINDNESS in the WORLD.

150

"Love grows when KINDNESS IS PLANTED."

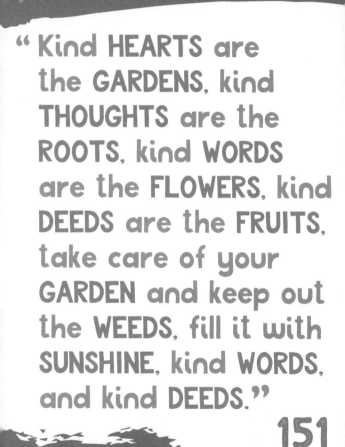

" Kind HEARTS are the GARDENS, kind THOUGHTS are the ROOTS, kind WORDS are the FLOWERS, kind DEEDS are the FRUITS, take care of your GARDEN and keep out the WEEDS, fill it with SUNSHINE, kind WORDS, and kind DEEDS."

151

" With just a little drop of kindness, you can water a whole garden. " **152**

Heather Wolf

153

" If speaking kindly to plants makes them grow, imagine what speaking kindly to humans can do. "

I reach for the sun like **154**

♪ **PLANTS DO**

(said with a big stretch up with your arms).

MAKE A DIFFERENCE

155

Who do you know that could do with a smile, or a friendly word, a hug or some of your time? Reach out in some way today and you could make all the difference. Be the light in their dark times.

"I wondered why somebody didn't do something. Then I realized, I am somebody." **156**

157

> **KINDNESS** can **TRANSFORM** someone's dark moment with a **BLAZE** of **LIGHT**. You'll never know how much your caring matters. Make a **DIFFERENCE** for another today.

Amy Leigh Mercree

I make a **DIFFERENCE.**

158

159

"As we work to create light for others, we naturally LIGHT our own way."

Mary Anne Radmacher

160

I am **KIND**
wherever and
whenever possible.

"Bring **LOVE** wherever you go. **SHINE LIGHT** wherever it is dark. Leave **BLESSINGS** wherever you have been. Be **KIND** wherever you are."

161

Mary Davis

Kindness to the Planet

162

♪

Here is a list of planet-kind activities for every day this week – how many can you tick off the list?

- Pick up 5 pieces of litter.
- Choose a toy to give to your local charity shop.
- Donate a book to someone you know will love it.
- Turn off the tap whilst you brush your teeth.
- Mend something.
- Walk or cycle instead of drive.
- Put out food for the birds.

163
I AM A PLANET PROTECTOR.

164
" He that plants trees loves others besides himself. "

Thomas Fuller

"YOU cannot get through a SINGLE DAY without having an impact on the WORLD around YOU. What you do makes a DIFFERENCE, and you have to decide what kind of a DIFFERENCE YOU want to make."

Jane Goodall

"Small acts, when multiplied by millions of people, can transform the world." **166**

" The world is a fine PLACE AND WORTH fighting for. " 167
Ernest Hemingway

I am kind to the
168 **EARTH.**

KINDNESS TO THE WORLD

169

Volunteering is when you give your time to helping with a cause. You could volunteer to help younger kids read at school, or to clear the leaves for an older neighbour. Giving your time and energy to help make a difference is truly a kind thing to do.

What could you volunteer to do this week?

170

I am a willing **VOLUNTEER**.

171

❝Unless someone like you cares a whole awful lot. Nothing is going to get better. It's not.❞

Dr. Seuss

172

"Let's stop waiting for a better world. Let's start working on it together."

173

"The PURPOSE of life is to CONTRIBUTE in some way to making things BETTER."

Robert F. Kennedy

I give **MY TIME** and **ENERGY** to **174** make things better.

175

"Don't **WAIT** for other **PEOPLE** to be loving, giving, compassionate, grateful, forgiving, generous, or friendly... lead the way!"

Steve Maraboli

Help

176

If you look carefully there will be people very close to you who need help with something. Perhaps dad's car needs cleaning, or your sister needs to learn how to tie her laces. Maybe your best friend is struggling with spelling, or your grandad has a problem working his iPad.
Pop on your superhero cape and go and save the day!

I am a good HELPER.

177

"If we always helped one another, no one would need luck."

Sophocles

178

179

" **NEVER WORRY** about numbers. **HELP** one **PERSON** at a time and always **START** with the **PERSON NEAREST YOU.**

Mother Teresa

"Never look down on anybody unless you're helping them up."
180   Jesse Jackson

" Always have a willing hand to help someone, you might be the only one that does. "
181   Roy T. Bennett

I reach out to **182**
PEOPLE IN NEED.

Talk Kindly to Yourself

183

You would (I hope) never dream of telling your friend they were rubbish if they missed shooting a basketball, or tell your sibling they were stupid if they found their homework hard. The reason you don't do that is because it is mean and would make them feel worse.

It works the same way if you talk to yourself meanly. So don't!

Have a little chat with yourself this morning and do the following:

- Say well done to yourself for something.
- Encourage and be gentle with yourself about something you are finding tricky.
- Remind yourself you are amazing and lovely.

Doesn't that feel good? Always try to talk to yourself with kindness and respect. It will make you feel so much better.

If you can't say anything nice about yourself, practise.

184

"Life becomes beautiful when you learn to be as good to yourself as you are to others."

185

I talk to myself like a good friend would. ♪

186

❝What we say to ourselves in the privacy of our own minds matters.❞
Marie Forleo

187

❝Be CAREFUL how you are TALKING to YOURSELF because you are LISTENING.❞
Lisa M. Hayes

I SPEAK KINDLY TO MYSELF.

188

189

" Talk to yourself like you would to someone you love. "

Brené Brown

KIND TO YOUR MIND

190

Kissing your brain. Have you ever heard of this? The idea is you kiss your fingertips and touch them to your busy brain whilst also saying thank you. To be kind to your mind you must first recognize how amazing it is and how sometimes it needs a rest. Will you kiss your brain today, and then will you let it rest? A little doodling or cloud watching or listening to some music are all great ways to have some busy brain down time.

191

"It's not about being good at something. It's about being good to yourself."

192

My **BRILLIANT** BRAIN can do **AMAZING** things.

193

" The first rule
of kindness is
to be kind to
yourself. "

" With your HEAD full of
BRAINS and your SHOES
full of FEET, you're too
SMART to go down any
not-so-good STREET. "
194   Dr. Seuss

195
I ALLOW MY
MIND TO REST.

196
Always be
KIND to your
BRILLIANT MIND.

Kind to Your Body

197

Put on your favourite tunes, wear ALL your party clothes and clear some space... today is the day for an amazing Kitchen Disco. Dancing almost always makes things better and your body will thank you for being so kind as to let it dance!

198
"DANCE LIKE NOBODY'S WATCHING."

♪

199
I treat MY BODY with love, friendship, and respect.

200

"SPEAK to your body in a LOVING WAY. It's the only one you've got, it's YOUR HOME, and it deserves YOUR RESPECT."

Iskra Lawrence

201 "You yourself, as much as anybody in the entire universe, deserve your love and affection."

202 "If you can't get a compliment any other way, pay yourself one."

Mark Twain

203 I am an awesome

DANCER ♪

(strike a dance pose as you say this).

KINDNESS EVERY DAY

204

Keep a kindness diary this week and record your daily acts of kindness each evening. How many did you squeeze into your 7 days?

"When is the best time to be kind? EVERYTIME."

205

206

KINDNESS makes my days LOVELY.

207

I TRY TO BE KIND EVERY DAY.

208

"How BEAUTIFUL a day can be when KINDNESS touches it!"

George Elliston

"Wake up. 209
Be kind. Repeat."

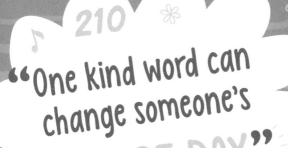

210

"One kind word can change someone's ENTIRE DAY."

Kindness is a
Strength

211

Sometimes kindness is easy
and fun and sometimes
it is hard and uncomfortable.
Do you know the story of Anne Frank
and the amazing lady that hid her
family during the war to keep them
safe? Miep Gies hid Anne's Jewish
family for years to protect them from
the Nazis. She helped them survive
by secretly bringing them food on a
daily basis even though it was very
dangerous for her to do so.
Kindness is a strength and reaching
in with kindness is always the answer
even when it is hard.
Can you think of any other examples
of when kindness requires
you to be strong?

212

★ MY ✿
KINDNESS
IS MY
STRENGTH.

♪

213

"In the **long** run, the **SHARPEST** weapon of all is a **kind** and gentle spirit."

Anne Frank

I can be kind even when it is hard. **214**

> "It is not genius, nor glory, nor love that reflects the greatness of the human soul; it is kindness." **215**
>
> Jean-Baptiste Henri Lacordaire

"You can ACCOMPLISH by KINDNESS what you cannot by FORCE. "

Publilius Syrus

"Your greatness
is not what
you have it is
what you give."

Alice Hocker

217

HANDLING UNKINDNESS

218

Can you recall a time someone was unkind to you, or you were unkind to someone else? Unkindness hurts. When someone is unkind to you it is important to make it stop as quickly as possible by speaking up or getting help. You deserve better. If it is you that is being unkind, catch yourself and change your behaviour. They deserve better. Make yourself a promise to do your best to stop unkindness in its tracks wherever possible.

219

I stand against **UNKINDNESS.**

220

" Hate cannot drive out hate: only love can do that. "

Martin Luther King Jr.

221

" What you do not want to be done to yourself, do not do to others. "

Confucius

222

" Our PRIME purpose in this LIFE is to HELP others. And if you can't help them, at LEAST don't HURT them. "

Dalai Lama

I treat people well.

223

224

"Never regret being a good person to the wrong people. Your kindness says everything about you. Their behaviour says everything about them."

Charity

225

My son raised enough money to fund the building of a whole classroom at a school in Malawi. He held a car boot sale, mowed lawns, and made cakes to sell and ran a quiz! My daughter raised £100 for a hospice by selling a fun magazine she created.

Which charity would you like to support and what could you do for them today? Could you ...

- fundraise?
- raise awareness by making a poster or giving a talk?
- donate your time to help?

Charities need people like you to help them and your support means they can spread their kindness far and wide.

I am eager to help.

226

"If you're feeling helpless, help someone."

Aung San Suu Kyi

227

228

"**HAPPINESS** doesn't result from what we get, but from what we give.

Ben Carson

> " We can change the world and make it a better place. It is in your hands to make a difference. "
>
> Nelson Mandela **229**

> " Do things for people not because of who they are or what they do in return, but because of who you are. "
>
> **230** Harold S. Kushner

♪ I give my **231** TIME AND ENERGY to good causes. ☆

What is Kindness?

232

How would you define kindness? Try and explain to someone or write a paragraph about what you think kindness is. Next ask 3 other people what they think kindness is. Is their definition similar to yours?

233
"Kindness is showing someone they matter."

234
I show people that I value them.

235

66 Kindness is more than deeds. It is an attitude, and expression, a look, a touch. It is anything that lifts another person. 99

Plato

236

66 Because that's what KINDNESS is. It's not doing something for someone else because they can't, but because you can. 99

Andrew Iskander

237

"KINDNESS IS LOVE IN ACTION."

238

I UNDERSTAND how important kindness is.

KINDNESS CHANGES THINGS

239

It is amazing how kindness changes things — today's mission is to be a secret kindness ninja. Spend today being your absolute kindest self, show kindness, and shower compliments, encouragement and good deeds on everyone you meet. At the end of your mission, ask yourself this:

Did kindness change today into one of the best days ever?

240

> " When you are kind to others, it not only changes you, it changes the world. "
>
> **Harold Kushner**

241

MY KINDNESS IS POWERFUL.

242

"To make a difference in someone's life you don't have to be brilliant, rich, beautiful, or perfect. You just have to care."

Mandy Hale

"Too often we underestimate the power of a touch, a smile, a kind word, a listening ear, an honest compliment, or the smallest act of caring, all of which have the potential to turn a life around."

243

Leo Buscaglia

244

I CARE.

245

To touch someone with KINDNESS is to change someone forever.

Mike Dooley

Kindness to Friendship

♪ **246**

There are many things we can do to help animals in need, such as leaving out a bowl of water for passing dogs on a hot day or calling up the local shelter and seeing if they need some pet food or blankets. Spiders sometimes need rescuing from bathrooms and setting free, and bees need us to plant flowers and fruits and herbs to feed them.

What could you do today to a help an animal in need?

247
I am kind to animals.

248
"Be kind to every kind, not just mankind."

Anthony Douglas Williams

249

"WE can JUDGE the HEART of a MAN by his TREATMENT of ANIMALS.

Immanuel Kant

> "The world was created for all of us not some of us."

250   Anthony Douglas Williams

251 "Just **BEE KIND!**"

♪ I **252** **APPRECIATE** every living thing.

WHAT GOES AROUND COMES AROUND

Cut colourful
paper into strips and
on each strip write a kind
action you have completed.
When you have finished, make it
into a circle and secure it with tape
or a staple.
Each circle is a symbol of how your
kindness will come back to you.
Turn your strips into a paper chain
and keep adding to it. How long will
it be by the end of the week – will
it stretch the length of your
bedroom wall?

253

254

"Kindness, like a boomerang, always returns."

255

I am GRATEFUL for all the KINDNESS I RECEIVE.

256

" If you want peace, be calm. If you want love, be loving. If you want kindness, be kind. "

Mary Davis

257

" LIFE is an ECHO. What you send out, comes back. What you SOW, you REAP. What you GIVE, you GET. "

Zig Ziglar

258

"When we give cheerfully and accept gratefully, everyone is blessed."

Maya Angelou

259

I SEND OUT KINDNESS EACH AND EVERY DAY.

A Kindness Trail

260

At the end of today make a little map of where you have been and mark off each place you were kind. Maybe you smiled at your neighbour, said thank you to your school receptionist, helped your teacher, or set out the goals at football training.
Put a little X to mark the spot where you left your little kindness mark on the world.

261
I make the
WORLD a
HAPPIER
place.

262
" Every act of
kindness is a
piece of love we
leave behind."
Paul Williams

263

"**EVERYWHERE** you go, leave a **GLITTER** trail of **KINDNESS** behind you."

"Spread kindness like confetti." 264

"Remember you're the 265 one who can fill the world with sunshine."

Snow White, *Snow White and the Seven Dwarfs*

I SCATTER 266 **KINDNESS** EVERYWHERE.

SMILE

267

A good joke or a kind word always make people smile.
Here's my best joke...
What do you call 2 robbers? A pair of knickers!
What's your best joke?

268

I have a big, beautiful smile.

"A smile is a friend maker."

269

Bangambiki Habyarimana

270

"Because of your SMILE, you make LIFE more BEAUTIFUL."

Thich Nhat Hanh

271

"A warm SMILE is the UNIVERSAL language of KINDNESS."

William Arthur Ward

I SMILE often. 272

273
"If you see someone without a SMILE, give them one of YOURS."

Kindness to Neighbours

274

Over a million older people say they go more than a month without speaking to a friend or family member. Have a chat about this with your family and ask yourself the following questions:

Does your family speak to your elderly neighbours and check they are ok? It could make all the difference. Have you shared your phone number in case they have a problem?

And what about your next-door neighbours – do you ever take them round cookies you have baked or perhaps you wheel their bin back up their drive on bin day?

What could your family do to be better neighbours?

275

I am a thoughtful neighbour.

"In order to have a good neighbour you have to be one."

Harry S. Truman

276

"**WHEN** one ☆
NEIGHBOUR helps
another, we
strengthen our
COMMUNITIES." ☆

Jennifer Pahlka

"All human beings are my neighbours. We share the same planet." **278**

Ana Monnar

"Wherever there is a human being there is an opportunity for kindness." **279**

280

I am a **FRIENDLY** neighbour.

We All Rise

281

When you smiled
at that stranger you
raised their day.
When you let your sibling choose
the game you raised their day.
When you gave your friend a
compliment you raised their day.
When you thanked your teacher
you raised their day.
When you gave yourself an encouraging
word you raised your own day.
Are you walking a little taller
when you think back on all your
kind deeds? We all rise
with kindness.

"We rise by lifting others."

My kindness SHINES brightly.

284

"The wonderful thing is that it's so incredibly easy to be kind."

Ingrid Newkirk

285

"KINDNESS is the light that DISSOLVES all walls between souls, families, and NATIONS."

Paramahansa Yogananda

" Be there for others but never leave yourself behind. "

286

Dodinsky

287

I lift other people up. (Show your muscles as you say this!)

YOU ARE AMAZING

288 Can we pause for a moment to appreciate you and all the fantastic kindness you share with the world? You are utterly amazing, and you make a huge difference.

Thank you. I appreciate you and the world does too.

Give yourself a hug and a high five and repeat after me. 'I am a kindness superhero, and I can change the world.' Way to go, you.

"Sometimes miracles are just good people with kind hearts."

KINDNESS is my SUPERPOWER.

291

"Treat everyone with politeness and kindness, not because they're nice, but because you are."

Roy T. Bennett

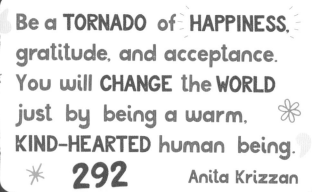

"Be a TORNADO of HAPPINESS, gratitude, and acceptance. You will CHANGE the WORLD just by being a warm, KIND-HEARTED human being."

292   Anita Krizzan

I AM UTTERLY FABULOUS. 293

294

"Not all SUPERHEROES wear capes."

When is it Hard to be Kind?

295

Sometimes it is hard to be kind even if you know it's important. When your friends are leaving someone out it can be hard to be the one that doesn't. If you see someone being bullied or someone being racist it can be hard to know what to do. Maybe you feel too young, too confused, too scared? Can you think of a time when it was hard to be kind?
Kindness isn't always easy, but it is always the answer. Dig deep. Ask for help if you need to, but be kind, always.

296

I am kind even when it's hard.

297

"Be kind to unkind people. They need it the most."

Dalai Lama

"**KINDNESS** in ourselves is the **HONEY** that **BLUNTS** the sting of **UNKINDNESS** in another."

Walter Savage Landor

"Weeds are flowers too once you get to know them." 299

I can ask **300** FOR HELP when I don't know what to do.

"Never lose a chance of saying a kind word."

301 William Makepeace Thackeray

SPREAD KINDNESS

Fill a bowl with water and grab a handful of tiny pebbles. Each time you are kind today pop a pebble to represent it into the water – the ripples you see show how your kindness will also ripple. If you smile at one person, they will more than likely smile at the next person they see, who might feel so good they open the door for a stranger, who might feel so happy they pick up some litter... and on and on and on. Kindness always spreads.

302

303

"Be kinder to yourself. And then let your kindness flood the world."

Pema Chödrön

304

I spread joy.

305

66 I alone cannot change the world, but I can cast a stone across the waters to create many ripples. 99

306

66 A SINGLE act of KINDNESS throws out roots in all directions, and the ROOTS SPRING up and make new trees. THE GREATEST work that KINDNESS does to others is that it makes them kind THEMSELVES. 99

Amelia Earhart

MY KIND WORDS AND ACTIONS REACH FAR AND WIDE. 307

308

"The very NATURE OF KINDNESS is to spread. If you are kind to others, today they will be kind to you, and tomorrow to SOMEBODY else."

Sri Chinmoy

WORLD KINDNESS DAY

309

World Kindness Day takes place on
13 November each year. It is celebrated across
the world and its aim is to create a kinder
world by inspiring individuals and nations
towards greater kindness.
It's party time – kindness is definitely worth
celebrating!
At school:
Can you talk to your teacher about your class
having a kindness party, or creating a display
of kindness stories to celebrate World Kindness
Day and inspiring each other?
At home:
Could you make a 'Happy World Kindness Day'
poster to display in your window and give
out little gifts of kindness throughout the day?
Isn't it amazing to think that around the
world on this day millions of other people are
intentionally being kind too in celebration of
World Kindness Day?

310

I celebrate
KINDNESS
every day.

311

"Astonish
the world
with your
kindness."

312

"In this WORLD where you have the OPPORTUNITY to be anything, BE KIND."

313

"Being deeply loved gives you strength; loving deeply gives you courage."

Lao Tzu

314
"The WORLD is full of KIND people, if YOU can't find one be one."

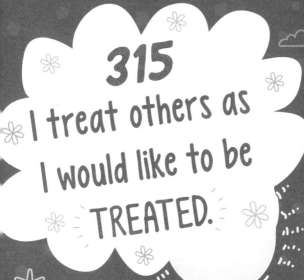

315
I treat others as I would like to be TREATED.

Random Acts of Kindness

☆ 316

A random act of kindness is an unexpected surprise — an act of kindness for no other reason than to be kind. They are often done for strangers, but you can also do them for people you know.

Here are some ideas:

- Leave a thank you note above your post box or on your dustbin.
- Make a playlist for your parents of all their favourite songs.
- Make wildflower seed bombs.
- Wash your family's or a neighbour's car.
- Make and take a parcel to a food bank.
- Write to your MP about something that could be better in your area.
- Make a simple bird feeder.
- Ask your local nursing home if someone might like a letter.
- Send a thank you message to your teacher.
- Help empty the dishwasher.
- Find some positive and happy quotes to put in your sibling's lunch box.

Which one will you do today?

317
I BRIGHTEN PEOPLE'S DAYS.

" Carry out a random act of **KINDNESS**, with no expectation of reward, safe in the **KNOWLEDGE** that one day **SOMEONE MIGHT** do the same for **YOU**. "

Princess Diana

I am THOUGHTFUL.

"The smallest act of kindness is worth more than the grandest intention."

321

"How do we change the world? One random act of kindness at a time."

Morgan Freeman

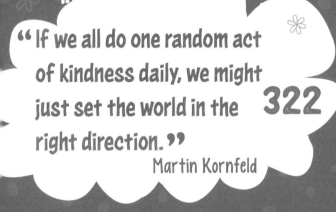

" If we all do one random act of kindness daily, we might just set the world in the right direction. "

322

Martin Kornfeld

Kindness Always Wins

323

If kindness was an athlete in the Olympic games, it would always win gold.
Can you (carefully) raid your recycling bin and create a kindness medal or trophy to remind you how kindness is always the winner?

324

I KNOW ✳ THAT ✳ KINDNESS WINS.

♪

"To err on the side of kindness is ☆ seldom an error."

Liz Armbruster

325

326

"I think probably KINDNESS is my number one attribute in a HUMAN BEING. I'll put it before any of the things like COURAGE, or BRAVERY, or GENEROSITY, or ANYTHING else... KINDNESS — that simple WORD. To be KIND — it covers everything, to my MIND. If you're KIND that's it."

Roald Dahl

"Do one act of kindness 327 each day of the year and change 365 lives."

Anthony Douglas Williams

"Simple kindness may be the most vital key to the riddle of how human beings can live with each other in peace, and care properly for this planet we all share."

328

Bo Lozoff ♪

I put
KINDNESS
first.
329

Kindness Superhero

330

Sometimes it might feel easier to not bother and to do nothing. But kindness is ALWAYS worth it. If you are going to be a kindness superhero you need to feel strong. Give these superhero power poses a try.

Strike a superhero pose by tipping your chin up. pushing your chest out. placing your hands on your hips and spreading your legs about hip length apart — hold it for 2 minutes.

OR

Try a 'V' pose by planting your feet apart and reaching your arms up into a V shape. This pose lets you breathe deeply and will help you feel calm and strong and ready to take on any kindness challenge.

I am STRONG. 331

"Accept the challenge of kindness." 332
Lady Gaga

333

A TRUE HERO isn't measured by the size of STRENGTH, but by the size of his HEART.

Zeus, Hercules

334

When you put LOVE out in the WORLD it travels, and it can touch people and reach people in ways that we never even EXPECTED.

Laverne Cox

I am a KINDNESS SUPERHERO. 335

336

"When WORDS are both true and kind, they can change the WORLD."

Jack Kornfield

PAYING ATTENTION

337

Sometimes the kindest thing you can do is really listen to someone. Practise on any older people in your life and ask them about their school days or hobbies when they were young. They will have some interesting stories to tell you. Listening well will help you feel more connected to the person you are listening to, and it will make you feel closer to them.

The end result of kindness is that it draws people to you.

Anita Roddick

I am a good
LISTENER.

340

"Listening is one of the loudest forms of kindness."

"Those who bring 341 SUNSHINE to the lives of others cannot keep it from THEMSELVES."

J. M. Barrie

I PAY ATTENTION TO OTHER 342 PEOPLE.

343
"LISTENING is often the only thing needed to HELP SOMEONE."

Accepting Kindness

☆ 344

It isn't always easy to ask for and accept help or to receive and say thank you for a compliment. Both things can make us feel embarrassed and awkward.

All we ever need to do is say thank you. Next time someone pays you a compliment, or offers you a hand, don't push them away but let them know you value and appreciate them.

Have a practice... ask someone to pay you a compliment. Give them a beaming smile and simply thank them when they do. Keep going till it becomes easy and till you are so full of compliments you feel MAGNIFICENT!

345

I CAN ACCEPT HELP.

346

"Accepting help is its own kind of strength."

Kiera Cass

347

"You have to love yourself or you'll never be able to accept compliments from anyone."

Dean Wareham

"Always give without remembering and always receive without forgetting." 348

☆ Brian Tracy

"In the end, only kindness matters." 349

☆ Jewel

I can

ACCEPT

350 compliments. ☆

INSPIRING
KINDNESS

351

Quotes and sayings can be powerful and inspirational too. The next few pages contain some of my favourite kindness quotes of all. Can you pick your 5 favourites out of the book and pop them on a card to a friend, or make a poster of them to display in your home? Let's work on inspiring everyone to be kinder.

352

I inspire others to BE KIND.

"Wherever you go, go with all your heart."

353

Confucius

354

"Make KINDNESS the NORM."

The Random Acts of Kindness Foundation

355

"In a WORLD where you can be ANYTHING, be KIND."

Jennifer Dukes Lee

356

"No greater gift there is, than a **GENEROUS HEART.**"

357

I will spread the KINDNESS MESSAGE far and wide.

Different Kinds of Kindness

358

There are many ways to be kind:
- Some people like you to help them.
- Other people like hugs.
- Many people like to receive gifts.
- Some people like you to give them your time.
- Others like you to give them a compliment or share encouraging words.

These different kinds of kindness are sometimes called love languages.
What's your favourite love language?
Could you put the above types of kindness in order of which you like best?
Do you think this will be the same for everyone?

359

MY HEART is full of KINDNESS. ♪

360

"A friend is a gift you give yourself."

Robert Louis Stevenson

361

"There are **SOULS** in this **WORLD** who have the **GIFT** of finding **JOY** everywhere and **LEAVING** it behind them when they **GO**."

Frederick William Faber

I am KIND in many **362** DIFFERENT WAYS.

" Those who are happiest are those who do the most for others. "

Booker T. Washington **363**

"How far that little candle throws his beams! So shines a good deed in a weary world."

William Shakespeare **364**

365

Take some time today to reflect back on the year and the powerful impact of kindness. What act of kindness towards you really made a difference? And what act of kindness that you did had the biggest effect?

every 4 years is a leap year so here is one extra for you!

"KINDNESS is FREE, sprinkle it EVERYWHERE."

Acknowledgements

7 *The Grinch*, © Universal Pictures (2018)

26 Austen, Jane, *Emma*, J Murray (1815)

142 Barrie, James M., *The Little White Bird*, Hodder & Stoughton (1902)

167 Hemingway, Ernest, *For Whom the Bell Tolls*, Jonathan Cape (1941)

171 Dr. Seuss, *The Lorax*, Random House (1971)

194 Dr. Seuss, *Oh, the Places You'll Go!*, Random House (1990)

262 Ascher, Ken and Williams, Paul, 'A Little Bit of Love', A&M Records (1974)

265 *Snow White and the Seven Dwarfs*, © Walt Disney Pictures (1937)

333 *Hercules*, © Walt Disney Pictures (1997)

349 Kilcher, Jewel, 'Hands', Atlantic (1998)